TRACE

Use pens to trace the dotted lines and finish the pictures in this section.

This is Arty Mouse.
He needs **2** round ears.
Trace **4** lines for his whiskers.

Fun in the snow

Help Arty Mouse's friends to pull their sledges up the hill.

Make a racetrack so the friends can have more fun.

Follow the paths

Help the friends to cross the page
and find the treats.

Join the dots to finish the picture.

Can you spot the lines that look like the ones on the opposite page?

Up and down

The balloons are rising.
Trace lines up from
the ground.

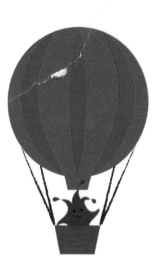

Trace the sun's rays, too!

The sun rises in the morning.

The balloons are falling.
Trace lines down from the sky.

The sun goes down in the evening.

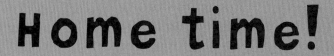

Home time!

Can you help these friends to find their way back home?

Trace the
wiggly paths
to our houses!

Spiro

Boat race

Trace the wavy lines in this boat race scene.

who do you think will win the race?

Shapes and colors
The Arty friends love shapes!
Can you help them to finish these?

Color the square red.

Color the circle green.

Color the triangle orange.

Color the rectangle purple.

Color the hexagon blue.

Snail race

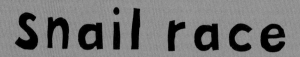

Spiro and his friends are
having a snail race!

Help the friends to find their way around the track.

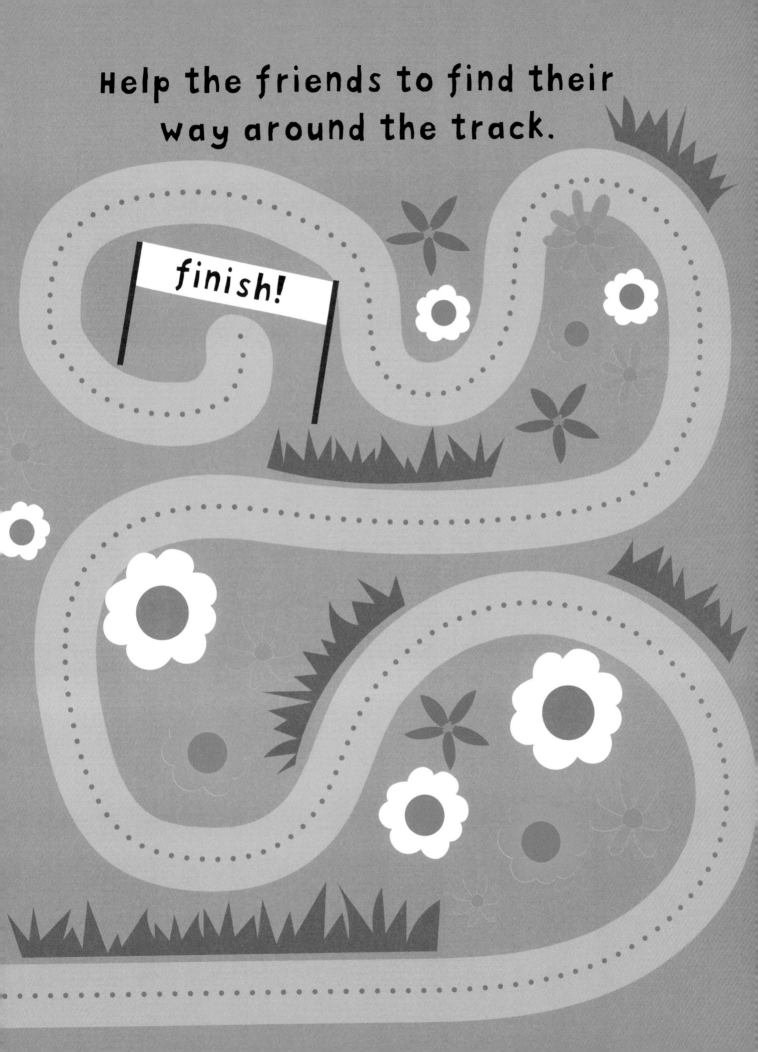

finish!

Arty's house

Arty Mouse and Geo are playing hide-and-seek! Finish the house so they can hide inside.

Arty's backyard is full of flowers. Trace the lines to finish them.

How many flowers can you count?

Goal!

Arty Mouse and his friends are playing soccer. It's so much fun!

Trace the goal, too!

How many balls are in the goal?

colorful fish

Scribble has drawn a picture, but the colors are missing!

Use matching colored pens or pencils to trace the lines from the crayons. Color the fish, too.

Spiral shells

Trace the circles to make shells
for Spiro's snail friends.

Spirals make me dizzy!

ski slope fun

Arty Mouse is skiing down
a mountain. Trace the lines
to show his trail.

Trace the
trees, too!

New sweater

Stripy is trying on his new sweater. Trace the dotted lines to finish the pattern.

Railroad puzzle

Arty Mouse needs to get to the station! Help him to drive his engine along the tracks.

Rainbow birds
Rainbow birds love color!

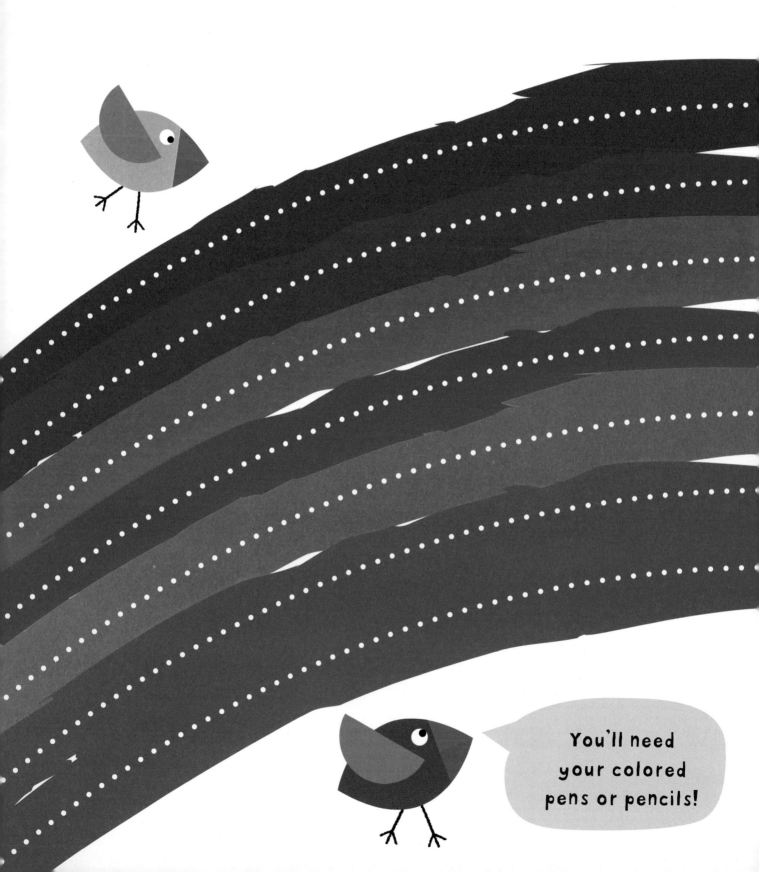

You'll need your colored pens or pencils!

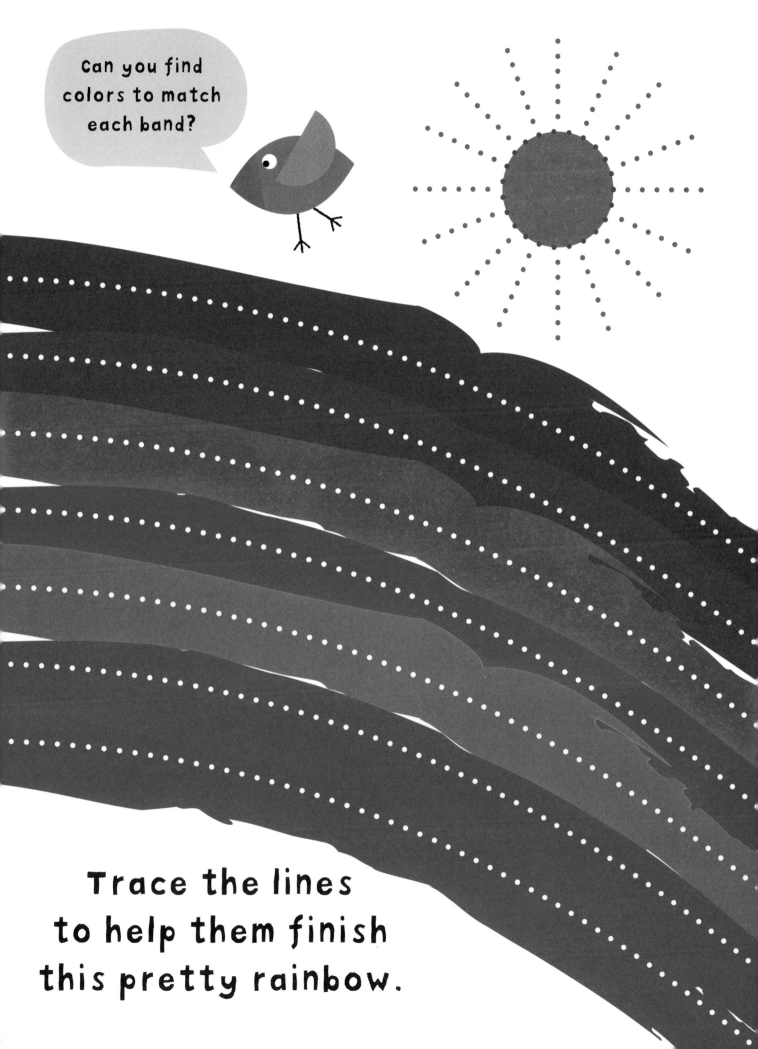

Monster fun!

Arty Mouse has seen something very strange! Trace the dotted lines to find out what it is.

Trace every dotted line to finish this monster scene!

Don't worry, I'm friendly! Please color me in.

Arty party

It's Arty Mouse's birthday.
Finish the balloons for party fun!

Amazing maze!
Help Arty Mouse to follow the trail of candies left by Stripy.

Can you draw a line that covers every candy?

Which way?

Arty Mouse has forgotten the way home. Can you help?

Look out for dead ends! I'm in a hurry.

Arty's house

A windy day

Arty Mouse and his friends
are flying kites.

Trace the strings to see
who each kite belongs to.

Trace in space

The Arty friends are
exploring in space.

Trace the dotted lines to find out which planet each friend visited.

Rockets travel really fast!

Shapes at the beach

There is something missing from this page...rectangles! Trace the lines to draw them all.

There is something missing from this page, too...circles! Can you trace them?

How many circles can you see?

Under the sea

Arty Mouse is exploring underwater. Trace the lines to finish the scene.

How many fish can you see?

Playtime

Stripy and Dot are playing in the ball pit. Can you trace around all of the balls?

Day and night

Scribble likes the day best...

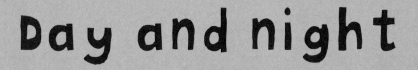

Trace the lines to finish the daytime things.

Rainbow chicks

Rainbow birds start life
as rainbow chicks.

Spider's web

This friendly spider needs help to complete his web. You'll have to concentrate!

This is tricky!

Jungle animals
Arty Mouse is exploring
in the jungle.

Can you help to trace all of the jungle animals?

Rainy day

Rain, rain, rain!
Finish the clouds, then
add the pouring rain!

I love jumping
in puddles!

Starry night

Trace the lines to discover who Dot can see in the stars.

Who does this look like?

Good night!

Make a colorful blanket to keep Arty Mouse warm. Good night, Arty Mouse!

Good night, everyone!

COPY

Use pens to draw over the dotted lines and copy the pictures in this section.

This is Arty Mouse.
Copy **1** ear and **2** whiskers.

Summer flowers

Arty Mouse loves flowers. Copy the petal shapes to finish the picture.

Finish these summer flowers, too.

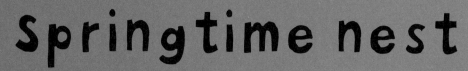

Bedtime!

Dot wants a sleeping bag
to match Stripy's.
Can you help to finish it?

Shapes fun

Geo loves shapes! Copy the shapes to finish each row.

Geo

Don't forget to color in your shapes!

Help Stripy to copy the shapes in the little house to make a big house.

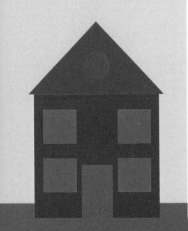

Scribble's fish

Scribble is looking at the fish's shapes.

Scribble

Copy my fish into the empty bowls.
Then color each one.

Happy robot

Copy the shapes to finish
the picture of Geo.

color in
the rest
of me!

Wonderful waves

Arty Mouse is having
fun in his boat.

Fill the sea with more wavy lines.

Scary waves!

Splat is sailing on the stormy sea.

Splat

Add more big waves, just like these!

Snail shells

Give every snail a spiral shell,
just like Spiro's.

Spiro

Lovely lollipops

Copy these lovely lollipop patterns
to finish Dot's treats.

Big bugs

Give the bugs black spots. Color around the spots with red.

Give me **5** spots!

Give me **6** spots!

Dot's flowers

Dot can see some pretty flowers. Fill her empty pot with flowers to match.

A flock of birds

Copy the rainbow bird's shape
to make a flock of birds.

Turn the shapes into
more rainbow birds!

Windy day

A windy day is perfect for flying kites.

Falling leaves

The birds are playing in the falling leaves.

Give every leaf a curly line.

Finish the friends

Copy Arty Mouse's finished half
to complete his picture.

Finish the picture
of Dot, too.

Ice cream treats

Help Arty Mouse and Stripy
to choose ice creams.

In the barn

Copy the cat's shape to make her **2** furry friends.

Meow!

1

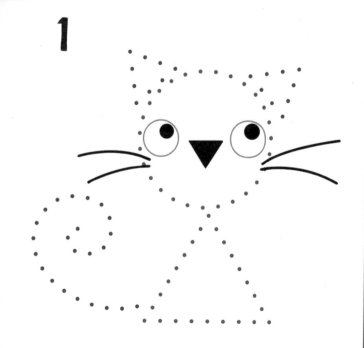

2

Copy the hen's shape to make her **2** feathery friends.

cluck! cluck!

1

2

Farmyard fun

Look closely at the blue cow.
Copy all the details to complete
the cow below.

Finish the pink pig, too.

Arty Street

Draw everyone a house with shapes like Arty's. Make each house different colors.

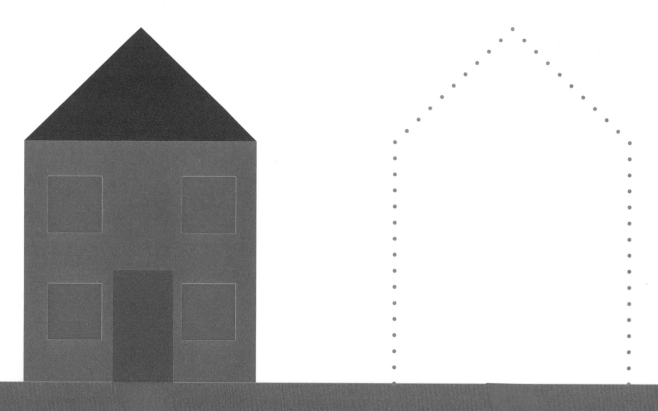

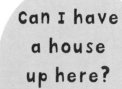

Can I have
a house
up here?

Add extra details
to make our
houses different.

Geo's candies

Can you help Geo to put candies in the empty jars?

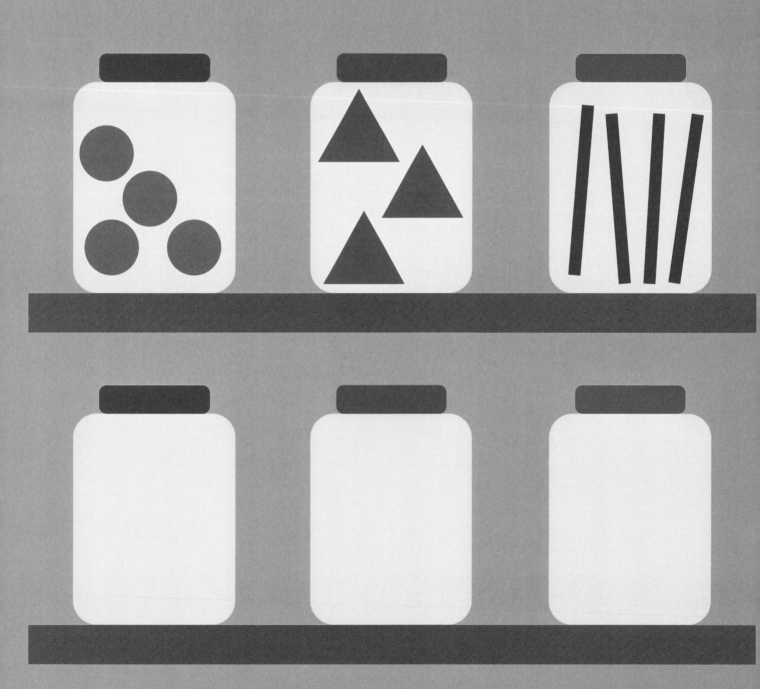

Copy the candies from the top jars into the matching jars below.

Geo's sandcastle

Geo loves making sandcastles.
Can you make one to match his?

Scribble's mirror

Use your pens or crayons to copy Scribble's reflection in the mirror.

Add scribbly lines to make fur like mine!

Painting Splat

Help Arty Mouse to paint Splat's portrait.

Birthday gifts

It's Stripy's birthday! Copy his pile of gifts in the empty space.

I wonder what this could be.

Can you copy more party flags?

Can you make each flag a different color?

Yummy picnic

What would each Arty friend like to eat?

You decide and copy it onto their plate.

Copy and count

Help Geo to fill his boxes with shapes.

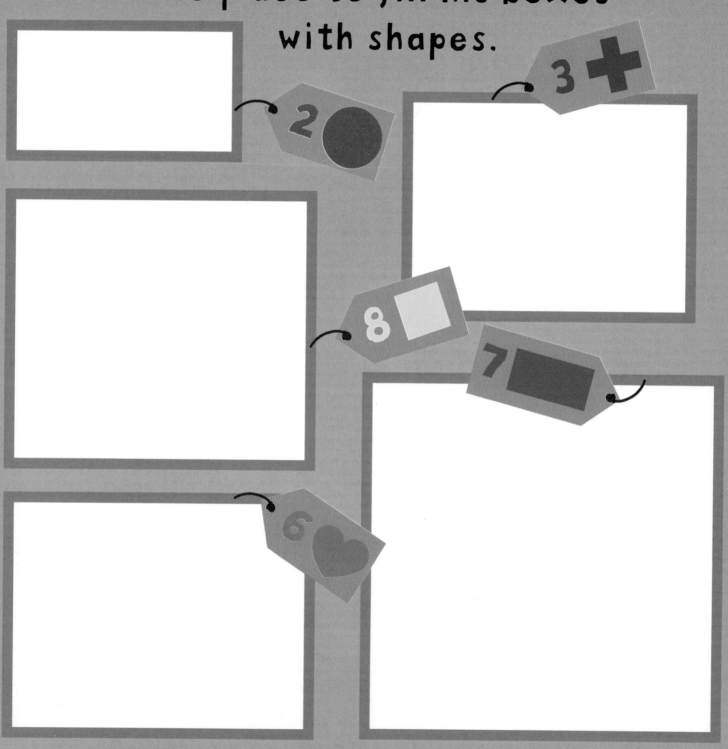

Look at the shape on the label, then copy the right number into each box.

Toy store

Copy each toy to fill the shelves.

Nighttime sky

Copy more star shapes into the sky and color them in. Then color the sky black.

COLOR

Use pens or pencils to color in the pictures in this section.

This is Arty Mouse.
Give him a red nose and gray ears.

Rainbow birds

Color each rainbow bird to match its outline. Pretty!

Helping friends

Dot is helping Arty Mouse to paint his house.

Spiro is busy in the backyard.

Creepy-crawlies

Finish the ladybugs by coloring around their spots in red.

This hungry caterpillar needs coloring in. Can you help?

Wash day

Splat is hanging out the washing. Color each T-shirt to match its outline.

Splat

Amazing maze

Color the trail to the middle of the maze. There's a treat waiting for Stripy!

stripy

Bird's nest

Mommy bird's nest is full of eggs.
Make each one a different color.

Arty's fruit bowl

Arty Mouse loves fruit! Can you color in these favorites?

what is your favorite fruit?

Train ride

Arty Mouse is driving his train.
Toot-toot!

Color the passenger cars in order...

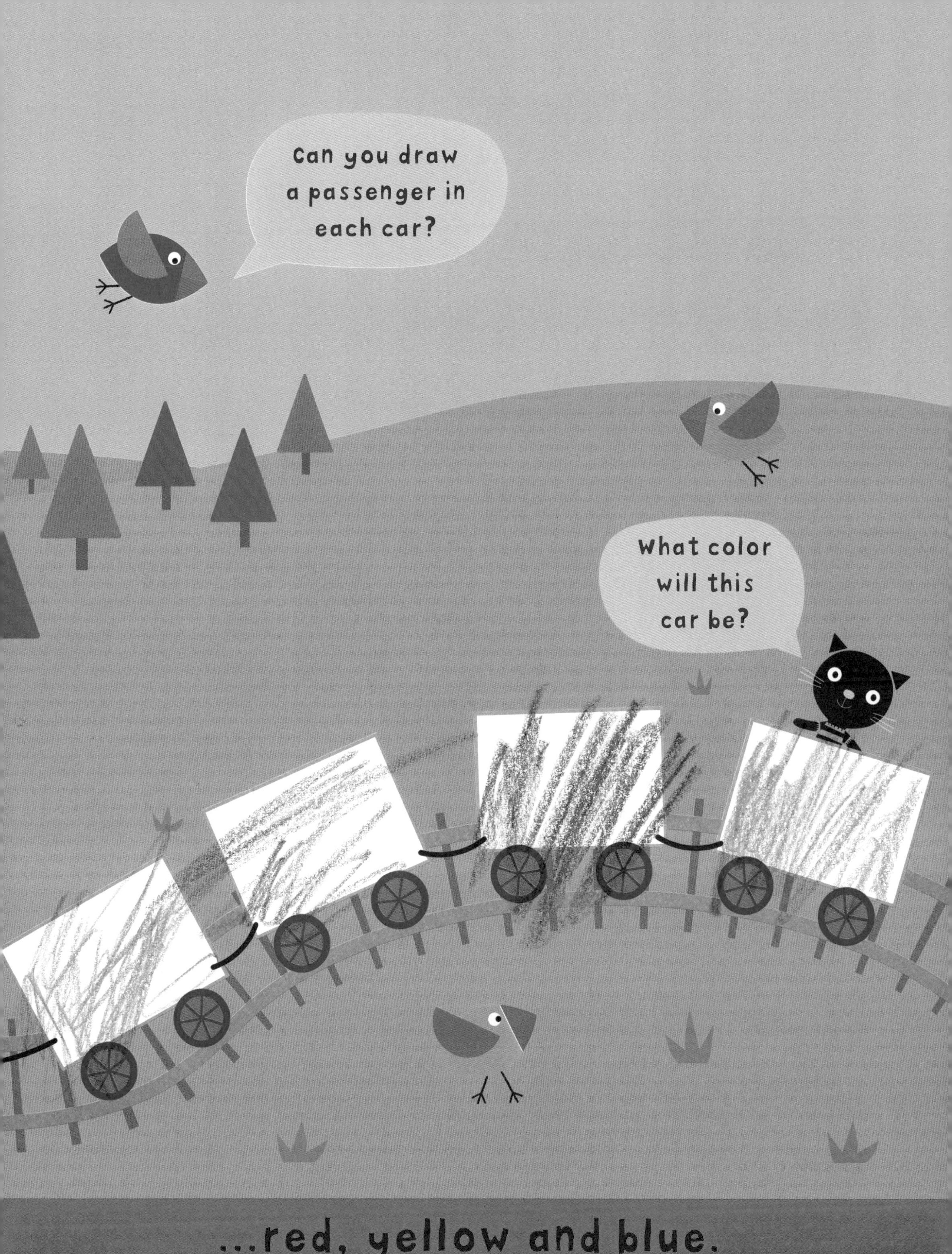

...red, yellow and blue.

Hide-and-seek snails

The snails are playing hide-and seek.
Color them to match the places
where they are hiding.

Flying high

The rainbow birds are playing chase. Color each trail to match the bird.

Arty artist

Arty Mouse has drawn a self-portrait.
Color it in to match the artist!

Rainy day

Today is rainy. Dot needs
a colorful umbrella
to keep her dry.

Use any colors
you like, but stay
inside the lines!

Sunny day

Today is sunny. Geo needs
a colorful umbrella
to keep him cool!

We love snow!

Playing in the snow is lots of fun!

color everything that isn't snow.

Party time!

The Arty friends are having a party!
Give everyone a matching
hat and balloon.

Baking day

Help Dot to decorate her cake.

Ice the cupcakes to match their cases.

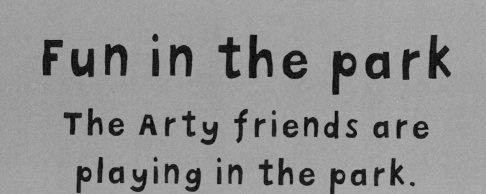

Can you finish coloring the scene?

Color the trees green.

Finish the frame and slide in pink.

Color the see-saw red.

Scribble's picture

Help Scribble to color in his flower picture.

Geo's wall

Geo is building a big wall.
Use the colors you can see
to help him finish it.

Phew!
Building is
hard work!

Beep-beep!

Arty Mouse and
his friends are
having a race.

VROOM!

Can you
spot who the
drivers are?

Color the cars to match their outlines.

At the aquarium

Splat has spotted the fish he was looking for. Color it in to match his picture.

stripy thinks the turtle is cool!

Make it any colors you like.

Vacation fun

The Arty friends are on vacation.
Can you finish coloring the scene?

Arty gallery

Arty Mouse and Stripy are looking at the pictures.

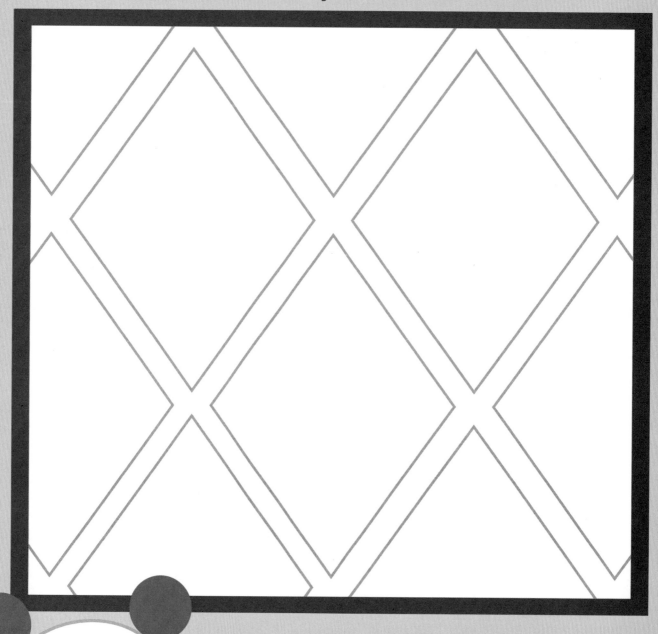

Wow! This picture is huge!

Fill in the pictures using any colors you like.

I like this one best.

Beautiful butterflies

Color a different pattern
on each butterfly.

Use two
colors for
each of us.

Scribble in space!

Scribble is exploring space in his rocket.

color all the amazing planets
and the twinkling stars.

On the farm

Spiro and Splat can see lots of animals in the field.

What colors will you use to finish each one?

Shopping trip

Scribble is at the grocery store.

Fill each shelf with matching food.

Sweet dreams!

What is Arty Mouse dreaming about? Draw your picture and color it in.

ZZZ...

CUT

This is Arty Mouse.
Cut a rectangle door shape so he
can visit his friends in Arty World.

Use scissors to cut
along the dotted
lines and finish the
activities in this
section.

Hello everyone!

Arty Mouse has found his friends. Cut along the dotted line to make the mountaintops.

Stripy

Scribble

Dot

Cut along the lines to make paths across the mountain.

Fun at the beach

Cut along the top of Spiro's amazing sandcastle.

spiro

Arty castle

Can you add windows to the castle?

Sailboats

Give every boat a sail so the
friends can sail away!

In the jungle

Spiro wants to play with the friendly crocodile.

Cut along his amazing teeth.

The snake
wants to join
in the fun.

Cut me out so I can
play, too.

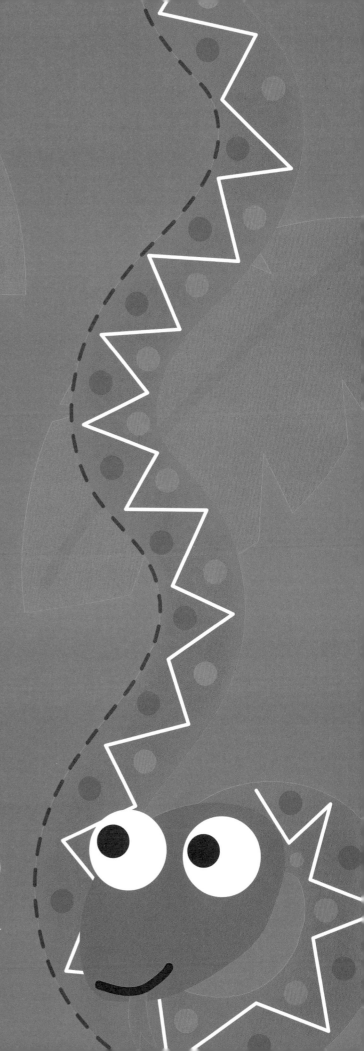

Underwater
Cut out the fish and put it in the water.

Scribble's quilt

Cut along the dotted lines
on Scribble's stripy quilt.

zzzz...

Cut along the dotted lines. Fold the stripes backward and forward.

Weave the top stripes in and out. Check out the other side!

In the barn

Spiro is talking to the hens.
Cut out the window and turn it
over to see who is outside.

Arty's picture

Cut out the shapes to help Arty make his picture.

splat

Flying high!

Cut along the dotted lines to each flying rainbow bird.

Snail trail

Cut along the dotted lines to make Spiro's snail trail.

Mouse hole surprise!

who is knocking at the door?
Cut it out and turn it over to see!

colorful rainbow

The birds love this colorful rainbow! Follow the dotted line to cut it out.

Kite flying fun

Give everyone a kite to
fly high in the sky.

Arty's engine

Can you help Arty Mouse to add rail cars to his engine?

How many rail cars can you fit behind me?

Mouse in space!

Cut out the triangles to complete Arty's amazing space rocket.

cut out the planets to finish
the space scene.

Sunny day!
Cut along the dotted lines
to make the sun shine.

Find Dot!
Help Scribble to find Dot by cutting along the dotted line.

Geo's wall

Cut out the
bricks and help
Geo to finish
building his wall.

Small waves

Stripy likes sailing on the calm sea.

Cut along the dotted lines
to make small waves.

Big Waves

Splat likes sailing on the rough sea!

Cut along the dotted lines to make big waves.

Fluffy cloud

Geo jigsaw
Cut out the shapes to finish Geo.

Where's my body?

Creepy-crawly caterpillar

Cut out the circles to finish the creepy-crawly caterpillar.

Dot's backyard

Snip all the dotted lines
to help Dot cut the grass.

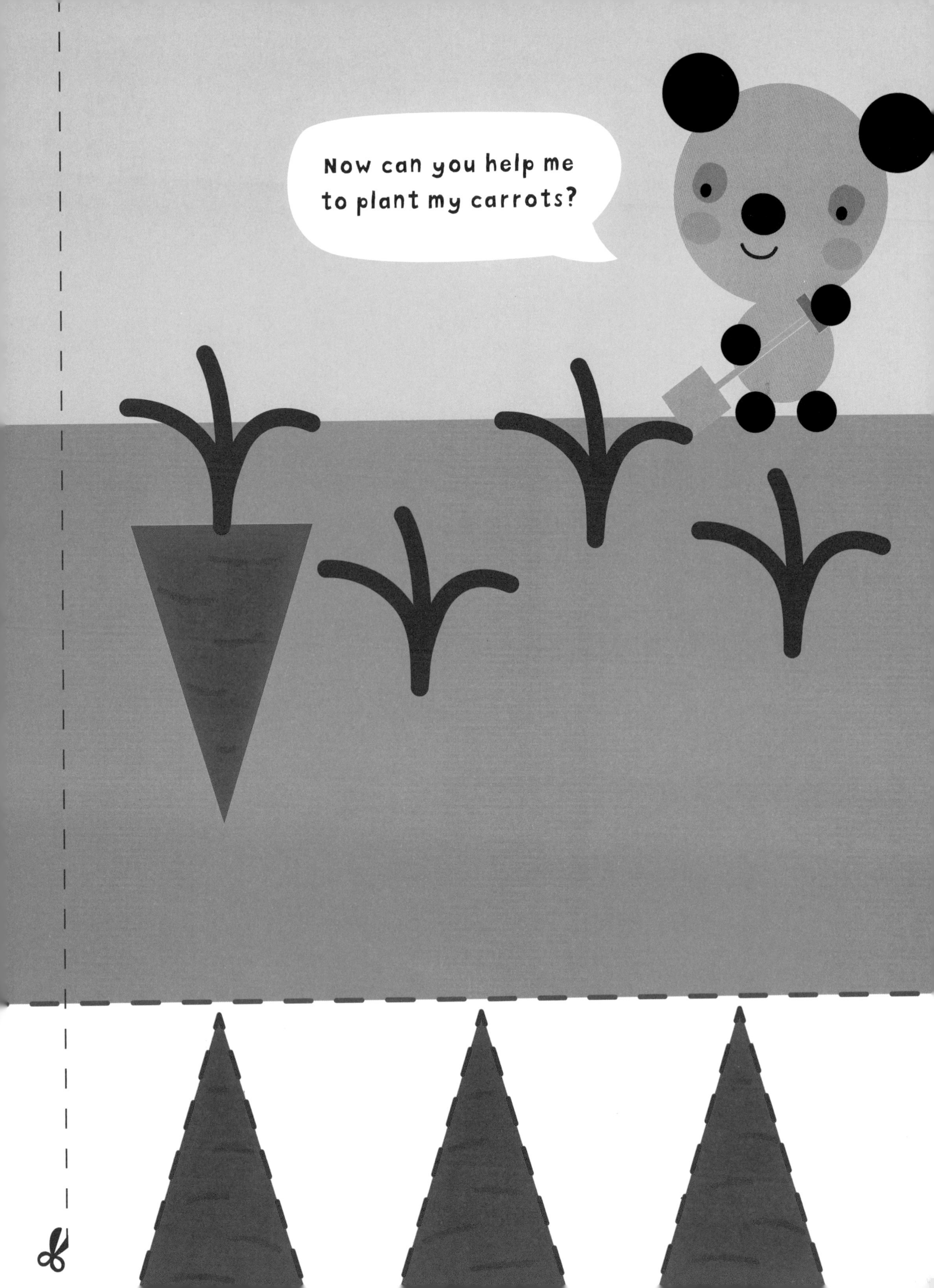
Now can you help me to plant my carrots?

Big city
The Arty friends are in the big city.

Who's inside?

Geo has seen a big tent. Cut out the door and turn it over to see who is on the other side.

Spiders' webs

Dot wants to find a new home
for her spider friends. Cut out
the webs and put them
somewhere nice and dry.

In the rain

Cut out the triangles to make
an umbrella for Scribble.

Nighttime window

Cut out the shapes. Then rearrange them in the window to see what Arty Mouse is doing.

Who's who?

Can you work out who the speech bubbles belong to?

Party hats

Give everyone a party hat to add to the fun!